Cover photographs capture the reuse of the Former Spellman Engineering Superfund site, the Midvale Slag Superfund site, and the Norwood PCBs Superfund site. See pages 22, 25 and 30 for additional site details. The Superfund Redevelopment Initiative has more information about these sites. The Brownfields and Land Revitalization Cleanup Enforcement website provides information about the liability protections that facilitated these projects.

Office of Site Remediation Enforcement/Office of Enforcement and Compliance Assurance

U.S. Environmental Protection Agency

June 2014

Table of Contents

List of Text Boxes, Highlights and Tables

Commonly Used Acronyms and Abbreviations

AAI	All Appropriate Inquiries
BFPP	Bona Fide Prospective Purchaser
Brownfields Amendments	Small Business Liability Relief and Brownfields Revitalization Act of 2002
CERCLA	Comprehensive Environmental Response, Compensation, and Liability Act
CPO	Contiguous Property Owner
DOJ	United States Department of Justice
MOA	Memorandum of Agreement
MOU	Memorandum of Understanding
NPL	National Priorities List
OSRE	Office of Site Remediation Enforcement
O&M	Operations and Maintenance
PLA	Prospective Lessee Agreement
PPA	Prospective Purchaser Agreement
PRP	Potentially Responsible Party
RCRA	Resource Conservation and Recovery Act
RfR	Ready for Reuse
SEP	Supplemental Environmental Project
SRI	Superfund Redevelopment Initiative
TSDF	Treatment, Storage, and Disposal Facility
UST	Underground Storage Tank
VCP	Voluntary Cleanup Program

Purpose and Use of the Revitalization Handbook

The U.S. Environmental Protection Agency's (the EPA) Office of Site Remediation Enforcement (OSRE) manages the enforcement of the nation's hazardous waste cleanup laws, including the Comprehensive Environmental Response, Compensation, and Liability Act (CERCLA, commonly known as Superfund), the corrective action and underground storage tank cleanup provisions of the Resource Conservation and Recovery Act (RCRA), and the Oil Pollution Act (OPA). The main objective of the cleanup enforcement program is to ensure prompt site cleanup and the participation of liable parties in performing and paying for cleanups in a manner that ensures protection of human health and the environment.

Both CERCLA and RCRA are designed to protect human health and the environment from the dangers of improperly disposed hazardous substances. The RCRA programs focus on how wastes should be managed to avoid potential threats to human health and the environment. CERCLA, on the other hand, applies primarily when contamination has already occurred, resulting in releases of hazardous substances to the environment. Both programs, however, have cleanup authorities that address contaminated sites.

Congress passed the Small Business Liability Relief and Brownfields Revitalization Act of 2002 (Public Law 107-118) (hereinafter, the Brownfields Amendments), which modified CERCLA and further promoted the cleanup, reuse, and redevelopment of sites by addressing liability concerns associated with unused or underutilized property. OSRE provides policy and guidance on the liability protections available to property owners and other parties as a result of the Brownfields Amendments and other federal laws governing the cleanup of contaminated land. OSRE plays a key role in land reuse and revitalization, including at brownfield sites, by providing guidance and developing tools that assist parties seeking to clean up, reuse, or redevelop contaminated properties.

OSRE is committed to encouraging site reuse to achieve enforcement and environmental protection goals, such as long-term site stewardship and sustainable land use planning. Often, reuse supports these enforcement and environmental protection goals and helps remove obstacles to cleanups and revitalization. Over the years, OSRE has highlighted these efforts through a series of handbooks, most recently in the 2011 *Revitalizing Contaminated Sites: Addressing Liability Concerns*. This 2014 edition of the handbook, *Revitalizing Contaminated Lands: Addressing Liability Concerns (The Revitalization Handbook)* is a compilation of enforcement tools, guidance, and policy documents that are available to help promote the cleanup and revitalization of contaminated sites.

This handbook summarizes the statutory, policy and guidance, and regulatory provisions that may be helpful to parties looking to manage environmental cleanup liability risks associated with the revitalization of contaminated sites. It is designed for use by parties involved in the assessment, cleanup, and revitalization of sites, and provides a basic description of the tools that may be available to address liability concerns.

For any party contemplating the revitalization of contaminated or formerly contaminated property, there are a number of important initial considerations and determinations. For example:

- A party should determine the end use of the property and should collect and consider information on past uses and potential contamination.

- If a party intends to purchase the property, it should consider whether it needs to conduct all appropriate inquiries (AAI) to take advantage of CERCLA liability protections, such as the bona fide prospective purchaser protection (BFPP).

- If a party needs information or has concerns about cleanup or liability protection, it should identify the most appropriate level of government to consult.

- A party may want to employ private mechanisms such as indemnification or insurance (see Private Party Tools text box), or take advantage of existing state tools, programs, or incentives such as participating in a state voluntary cleanup program.

- If contamination on the property warrants the EPA's attention under CERCLA or RCRA, a party should first determine if the EPA or the state is taking or planning to take action at the property. After determining where the property fits in the federal or state cleanup pipeline, a party may use this handbook to help decide which tools, if any, may be most appropriate.

Though prospective purchasers, developers, and lenders may hesitate to get involved with contaminated properties because they fear that they might be held liable under CERCLA or RCRA, many contaminated properties may never be subject to the EPA's attention under CERCLA, RCRA, or any other federal law. Perceived fears of federal involvement rather than the EPA's actual practice are often the primary obstacles to the redevelopment and reuse of brownfields. The EPA hopes that this handbook will provide a better understanding of these laws and their implementation.

DISCLAIMERS

This handbook is intended to provide general information to assist with the reuse of properties. This handbook is not legally binding. The word "should" and other similar terms used in this handbook are intended as general recommendations or suggestions that might be generally applicable or appropriate and should not be taken as providing legal, technical, financial, or other advice regarding a specific situation or set of circumstances. This handbook is not a rule and it does not create new liabilities or limit or expand obligations under any federal, state, tribal, or local law. It is not intended to and does not create any substantive or procedural rights for any person at law or in equity. In addition, this handbook does not alter the EPA's policy of not providing "no action" assurances outside the context of a legal settlement or formal enforcement proceeding.

This handbook discusses EPA guidance documents which may address the exercise of its enforcement discretion on a site-specific basis where appropriate. This handbook does not address all the circumstances in which the EPA may choose to exercise enforcement discretion with respect to a party under CERCLA, nor does it cover all of the statutory or other protections that may be available to a party at contaminated or formerly contaminated property. This handbook does not modify or supersede any existing EPA guidance document or affect the EPA's enforcement discretion in any way.

I.   Overview of CERCLA and RCRA

A.   CERCLA

In 1980, in response to public concern about abandoned hazardous waste sites such as Love Canal, Congress enacted CERCLA, which authorizes the federal government to assess and/or clean up contaminated sites and provides authority for emergency response to releases of hazardous substances.

CERCLA establishes a comprehensive liability scheme to require certain categories of parties to conduct or pay for cleanup of such releases. The EPA may exercise its response authority through removal or remedial actions. Remedial responses financed by the Hazardous Substance Trust Fund are undertaken only at sites on the EPA's National Priorities List (NPL). The National Contingency Plan (NCP), 40 C.F.R. Part 300, provides the "blueprint" for conducting removal and remedial actions under CERCLA.

There are many different types of contaminated or potentially contaminated property in the United States. Some may be "Superfund sites"-- sites where the federal government is, or plans to be, involved in cleanup efforts. Many of these sites are listed on the NPL. Other properties may be "brownfields"--properties where expansion, redevelopment, or reuse may be complicated by the presence (or potential presence) of contamination. The level of contamination may vary. Often, the federal government is not involved in cleanups at brownfield sites. Rather, state and tribal response programs play a significant role in cleaning up and helping to revitalize these sites. Other contaminated properties may be "RCRA brownfields" - RCRA facilities where reuse or redevelopment is slowed due to real or perceived concerns about requirements imposed by RCRA for actual or potential contamination.

The EPA launched the Brownfields Initiative in the mid-1990s and developed guidance and tools to help further the Initiative's goals to empower states, communities, and other stakeholders to assess, safely clean up, sustainably reuse, and prevent future brownfield sites. Congress codified many of the EPA's Brownfields Initiative practices, policies, and guidances into CERCLA when it passed the Small Business Liability Relief and Brownfields Revitalization Act of 2002 (Public Law 107-118) (Brownfields Amendments). The 2002 amendments to CERCLA defines a brownfield site as "real property, the expansion, redevelopment, or reuse of which may be complicated by the presence or potential presence of a hazardous substance, pollutant, or contaminant." CERCLA § 101(39).

CERCLA also includes provisions to:

- Address the liability concerns of certain landowners;

- Provide statutory authority for the EPA's brownfields grant program;

- Enable the EPA to obtain a windfall lien on certain properties owned by bona fide prospective purchasers; and

- Prohibit certain EPA enforcement at most brownfields sites being addressed under state response programs.

Under CERCLA's liability scheme, the current owner of a contaminated property is responsible for the property's cleanup based solely on its ownership status, even if the owner did not contribute to the contamination. As a result, entities that want to purchase contaminated properties are often concerned about incurring CERCLA liability once they acquire the property. To address these liability concerns, the Brownfields Amendments included new liability protections (and clarified the existing innocent landowner protection) for landowners who acquire property and meet certain criteria both before and after acquisition.

U.S. Environmental Protection Agency
Office of Site Remediation Enforcement

The three categories of landowners addressed in the Brownfields Amendments are:

- Bona fide prospective purchasers (BFPPs);

- Contiguous property owners; and

- Innocent landowners.

These landowner liability protections, the CERCLA liability scheme, and related cleanup enforcement policy and guidance are discussed in Section III.

The Superfund enforcement program, Superfund cleanup program, Superfund Redevelopment Initiative, and Brownfields and Land Revitalization websites provide further information.

B.   RCRA

In 1976, Congress enacted the Resource Conservation and Recovery Act (RCRA), 42 U.S.C. §§ 6901 et seq., which authorizes the EPA to establish programs to regulate hazardous waste (Subtitle C), solid waste (Subtitle D), and underground storage tanks (Subtitle I). RCRA's goals include:

- Protecting human health and the environment from hazards posed by waste disposal;

- Conserving energy and natural resources through waste recycling and recovery;

- Reducing the amount of waste generated; and

- Ensuring that wastes are managed in an environmentally safe manner.

Through RCRA Subtitle C, Congress gave the EPA the authority to manage hazardous waste from "cradle to grave." There are Subtitle C regulations for the generation, transportation, and treatment, storage, or disposal of hazardous waste. These regulations first identify the criteria to determine which solid wastes are hazardous, and then establish various requirements for the three categories of hazardous waste handlers: generators; transporters; and treatment, storage, or disposal facilities (TSDFs). In addition, the Subtitle C regulations set technical standards for the design and safe operation of TSDFs. These regulations for TSDFs serve as the basis for developing and issuing permits, which TSDFs are required to obtain. Unlike CERCLA, RCRA does not contain a bona fide prospective purchaser or similar liability protection.

RCRA Subtitle I authorizes the EPA to establish a regulatory program that includes technical requirements to prevent, detect, and clean up releases from underground storage tanks (UST). Tanks that are subject to Subtitle I regulations may be found at a variety of locations, including convenience stores, service stations, small and large manufacturing facilities, and airports. Since the UST program is not part of RCRA Subtitle C, there are separate technical and administrative requirements, including notification, design and installation standards, and closure.

The RCRA state authorization program, the RCRA corrective action cleanup enforcement program, and Office of Underground Storage Tank websites provide further information.

II. Liability

A. CERCLA Liability

CERCLA's liability scheme ensures that wherever possible, potentially responsible parties (PRPs), rather than the general public, pay for cleanups (often referred to as the "polluter pays principle"). As described in CERCLA § 107(a), the following categories of persons may be held liable for the costs or performance of a cleanup under CERCLA:

(1) The current owner or operator of a facility;

(2) An owner or operator at the time of disposal;

(3) A person who arranged for the disposal or treatment of hazardous substances (generator or arranger); and

(4) A person who accepted a hazardous substance for transport to a disposal or treatment facility or to a site and such person selected the facility or site.

Under CERCLA's comprehensive liability scheme, a PRP's liability for cleanup is:

- Strict - A party is liable if it falls within one of the above categories in CERCLA § 107(a) regardless of whether its conduct was negligent, intentional, or in compliance with industry standards.

- Joint and Several - If two or more parties are responsible for the contamination at a site, any one or more of the parties may be held liable for the entire cost of the cleanup, regardless of its share of the waste contributed, unless a party can show that the injury or harm at the site is divisible.

- Retroactive - A party may be held liable even if the hazardous substance disposal occurred before CERCLA was enacted in 1980.

The EPA has adopted an "enforcement first" policy throughout the Superfund cleanup process to compel those responsible for contaminated sites to take the lead in cleanup, thus conserving taxpayer money for cleanups at sites where there are no financially viable PRPs. Using the enforcement authorities provided by Congress, the EPA may enter into settlements with or compel PRPs to cleanup a site where a release of hazardous substances has occurred. When the EPA spends Hazardous Substance Trust Fund monies to finance a removal or remedial action, the EPA may then seek reimbursement from PRPs. Private entities may also conduct cleanups and seek reimbursement of eligible response costs from PRPs.

Many Diversified Interests, Inc. (MDI) – Houston, Texas

The EPA placed the 36-acre Many Diversified Interests, Inc. (MDI) Superfund site on the NPL in 1999. With site ownership in the hands of a bankruptcy trustee and an EPA lien on the site to recover past site costs, it appeared unlikely that any party would step in to purchase or clean the site. To support reuse, EPA Region 6 implemented an Agreed Order on Consent and Covenant Not to Sue, the first-ever agreement between the EPA and a non-liable party for the cleanup of a Superfund site. The U.S. Department of Justice's regional and headquarters offices were involved throughout the process, representing the EPA during the site's bankruptcy proceedings and advising on legal aspects of the Agreed Order.

U.S. Environmental Protection Agency
Office of Site Remediation Enforcement

B.   RCRA Liability

Under RCRA Subtitle C, the EPA has developed a comprehensive program to manage hazardous waste. The program prevents future environmental problems from being caused by hazardous waste. In addition, it oversees the cleanup of current environmental problems caused by the mismanagement of waste. This cleanup process is known as "corrective action." The EPA possesses several corrective action authorities to compel cleanup. Owners and operators of facilities where releases have occurred are required to clean up contamination caused by the mismanagement of wastes. The box below displays the components of the corrective action process. Since the steps necessary to achieve cleanup at a facility depend on site-specific conditions, the corrective action process is flexible. The components may occur in any order, and not every component is necessary to determine that no further action is required.

States are an integral part of the RCRA program. The EPA may approve a state or territory's RCRA program to operate in lieu of the EPA's program. The EPA generally approves a state-administered RCRA corrective action program if the state requirements are no less stringent than the federal requirements and the state has the ability to take adequate enforcement actions. In authorized states, facilities must comply with the authorized state requirements rather than the corresponding federal requirements. After authorization, both the state and the EPA have the authority to enforce those requirements.

Currently, 50 states and territories have been granted authority to implement the RCRA base, or initial, program, and 42 states and the territory of Guam are authorized to operate the RCRA corrective action program in lieu of the EPA's program. Owners and operators of corrective action sites in authorized states should contact their state regulatory agency because the state program may have different or more stringent requirements than the federal RCRA corrective action program.

More information is available on the RCRA state authorization program website and the RCRA corrective action cleanup enforcement program website.

COMPONENTS OF THE RCRA CORRECTIVE ACTION PROCESS

- Initial Site Assessment (RCRA Facility Assessment);
- Release Assessment and Site Characterization (RCRA Facility Investigation);
- Interim Actions to control or abate ongoing risks to human health and the environment (Interim Measures);
- Evaluation of different alternatives to remediate the site (Corrective Measures Study);
- Remedy selection for a thorough cleanup of the hazardous release (Statement of Basis); and
- Design, construction, operation, maintenance, and monitoring of the chosen remedy (Corrective Measures Implementation).

III. Statutory Protections and the EPA's Enforcement Policies and Guidance for the Cleanup, Reuse, and Revitalization of Contaminated Sites

The Office of Site Remediation Enforcement (OSRE) in the EPA's Office of Enforcement and Compliance Assurance is charged with enforcing CERCLA, RCRA corrective action, underground storage tank cleanup requirements, and aspects of the Oil Pollution Act, 33 U.S.C. § 2701 et seq. In this capacity, OSRE began to develop a comprehensive approach in the early 1990s to provide enforcement guidance on liability issues under these statutes to assist with the reuse and revitalization of contaminated property.

Partly in response to the EPA's efforts, Congress enacted the Brownfields Amendments, which amended CERCLA by adding new landowner liability protections (and clarifying the existing innocent landowner protection) and by providing funding for grants for the assessment and cleanup of brownfields. Since enactment of the Brownfields Amendments, OSRE has developed guidance documents, model enforcement documents, responses to frequently asked questions, fact sheets, and other documents to support revitalization of contaminated land. The EPA's Superfund enforcement website contains brownfields policy and guidance documents.

A. Statutory Defenses and Liability Protections

1. Bona Fide Prospective Purchasers

Before 2002, prospective purchasers of contaminated property could not avoid the CERCLA liability associated with being the current owner if they purchased with knowledge of contamination, unless before acquisition they entered into a prospective purchaser agreement (PPA) with the EPA that included covenants not to sue under CERCLA §§ 106 and 107. The 2002 Brownfields Amendments dramatically changed the CERCLA liability landscape by creating a new liability protection for a bona fide prospective purchaser (BFPP). A key advantage of the BFPP protection is that it is self-implementing and, therefore, the EPA is not required to make determinations as to whether a party qualifies for BFPP status. A party can achieve and maintain status as a BFPP without entering a PPA with the EPA, so long as that party meets the statutory criteria.

Section 107(r) protects a party as a BFPP from owner/operator liability if the party acquires property after January 1, 2002, and meets the criteria in CERCLA § 101(40) and § 107(r). These criteria include the performance of "all appropriate inquiries" (AAI) before acquiring the property. In addition, a person wishing to assert BFPP status cannot otherwise be a PRP at the site or have a prohibited "affiliation" with a liable party at the site. For parties seeking BFPP status, additional obligations throughout the period of ownership must be satisfied which include:

- Complying with land use restrictions and not impeding the effectiveness or integrity of institutional controls;

- Exercising appropriate care with respect to hazardous substances found at the property by taking "reasonable steps" to stop any continuing release and to prevent any threatened future release;

- Providing cooperation, assistance, and access;

- Complying with information requests and administrative subpoenas; and

- Providing legally required notices. CERCLA § 101(40).

BFPPs also must not impede the performance of a response action or natural resource restoration. CERCLA § 107(r).

BFPPs are not liable as owners/operators for CERCLA response costs, but the property they acquire may be subject to a windfall lien where the EPA's response action has increased the fair market value of the property. The United States, after spending taxpayer money for cleanup at a property, may have a windfall lien on the property for the lesser of the unrecovered response costs or the increase in fair market value at the property attributable to the Superfund cleanup. The windfall lien provision, which is found in CERCLA § 107(r), does not supplant the lien provision found in CERCLA § 107(*l*). For more discussion of resolution of windfall liens, please refer to Section IV.B.3.

BFPP PROTECTIONS MAY APPLY TO TENANTS

Leasehold interests play an important role in facilitating the cleanup and reuse of contaminated properties. Under current CERCLA case law, the mere execution of a lease does not necessarily make a tenant liable as an owner or operator under CERCLA § 107(a). The EPA recognizes the uncertainty regarding the potential liability of tenants under CERCLA and the potential applicability of the BFPP provision in light of the explicit reference to tenants in CERCLA § 101(40).

In 2012, EPA published its *Revised Enforcement Guidance Regarding the Treatment of Tenants Under the CERCLA Bona Fide Prospective Purchaser Provision.* This guidance discusses the potential applicability of the BFPP provision to tenants who lease contaminated or formerly contaminated properties, and how EPA intends to exercise its enforcement discretion on a site-specific basis to treat certain tenants as BFPPs under CERCLA.

This guidance discusses tenants who may derive BFPP status from an owner who is a BFPP. Further, EPA, on a site-specific basis, intends to exercise its enforcement discretion not to enforce against:

- A tenant of an owner who has lost BFPP status, if the tenant meets the elements of the BFPP provisions in CERCLA §§ 101(40)(A)-(H) and 107(r)(1) with the exception of the AAI provision; and

- A tenant who meets the elements of the BFPP provisions in CERCLA §§ 101(40)(A)-(H) and 107(r)(1).

In 2003, the EPA and the Department of Justice (DOJ) jointly issued *Interim Enforcement Discretion Policy Concerning "Windfall Liens" Under Section 107(r) of CERCLA*. The EPA separately published the accompanying *"Windfall Lien" Guidance Frequently Asked Questions*. In addition to explaining how the EPA intends to perfect the windfall lien and when the EPA may seek to foreclose on this lien, the guidance includes two attachments: (1) a sample "comfort letter" that explains to the recipient whether the EPA believes there is a possible windfall lien applicable to the property; and (2) a model settlement document, which the EPA may use to settle any applicable windfall lien provision in exchange for monetary or other adequate consideration.

In 2008, the EPA issued another windfall lien guidance, titled *Windfall Lien Administrative Procedures* and the associated *Model Notice of Intent to File a Windfall Lien Letter*. These documents provide guidance on the timing for filing notice of a windfall lien on a property and the EPA administrative procedures that should accompany filing a windfall lien notice.

2. **Owners of Property Impacted by Contamination from an Off-Site Source**

i. **Contaminated Aquifers**

Owners of property above aquifers contaminated from an off-site source may be concerned about CERCLA liability even though they did not cause and could not have prevented the ground water contamination. The EPA issued enforcement discretion documents before and after the Brownfields Amendments to address liability protections for contiguous landowners.

In 1995, OSRE developed the *Final Policy Toward Owners of Property Containing Contaminated Aquifers* in response to this concern. The EPA stated that it would not require cleanup or the payment of cleanup costs if the landowner did not cause or contribute to the contamination. It also stated that if a third party sued or threatened to sue, the EPA would consider entering into a settlement with the landowner covered under the policy to prevent third party damages being awarded.

The policy identifies certain exceptions when the policy will not be applicable, including, among others, when a well on the property may affect the migration of contaminants or when there is a contractual relationship between the landowner and the person causing the off-site contamination. In addition, the policy requires that the landowner must not be liable based on some other connection to the site, such as being a generator or transporter.

THRESHOLD CRITERIA FOR THE EPA'S CONTAMINATED AQUIFER POLICY

A landowner may be covered by the 1995 Contaminated Aquifer Policy. The EPA will exercise its discretion or may enter into a settlement if all the following criteria of policy are met:

- The hazardous substances contained in the aquifer are present solely as the result of subsurface migration from a source or sources outside the landowner's property;
- The landowner did not cause, contribute to, or make the contamination worse through any act or omission on his part;
- The person responsible for contaminating the aquifer is not an agent or employee of the landowner and was not in a direct or indirect contractual relationship with the landowner (exclusive of conveyance of title); and
- The landowner is not considered a liable party under CERCLA for any other reason such as contributing to the contamination as a generator or transporter.

This policy may not apply in cases where:

- The property contains a ground water well that may influence the migration of contamination in the affected aquifer; or
- The landowner acquires the property, directly or indirectly, from a person who caused the original release.

Fairchild Semiconductor Corp. (Mountain View Plant) – Mountain View, California

The 56-acre Fairchild Semiconductor Corp. (Mountain View Plant) Superfund site is located in Mountain View, California. The site is part of the Middlefield-Ellis-Whisman (MEW) Study Area, which also includes the Raytheon Company Superfund site, the Intel Corp. Mountain View Superfund site, and portions of the former NAS Moffett Field Superfund site. In 1989, the EPA issued a cleanup plan to address soil and ground water contamination across the MEW Study Area. A PPA between the EPA and a developer helped facilitate the purchase and redevelopment of more than 38 acres of the Fairchild Semiconductor site by 1998. Google Inc. now operates facilities at a number of properties at the Fairchild site.

ii. Contiguous Property Owners

The Brownfields Amendments added a statutory protection for contiguous property owners. Specifically, CERCLA § 107(q) excludes from the definition of "owner or operator" a person who owns property that is "contiguous," or otherwise similarly situated to, a facility that is the only source of contamination found on the person's property. Like the contaminated aquifer policy, this provision protects parties that are victims of contamination caused by a neighbor's actions.

To qualify as a statutory contiguous property owner, a landowner must meet the criteria set forth in CERCLA § 107(q)(1)(A). A contiguous property owner must perform AAI before acquiring the property and demonstrate that it is not affiliated with a liable party (see the text box on affiliation requirements). Like BFPPs, contiguous property owners must also satisfy ongoing obligations. Persons who know, or have reason to know, before purchase that the property is or could be contaminated cannot qualify for the contiguous property owner liability protection. These parties, however, may still be entitled to rely on the BFPP statutory protection or the EPA may exercise its enforcement discretion not to pursue such persons as set forth in the EPA's 1995 Contaminated Aquifer Policy.

In 2004, the EPA issued its _Interim Enforcement Discretion Guidance Regarding Contiguous Property Owners_ (Contiguous Property Owner Guidance), which discusses CERCLA §107(q). The guidance addresses:

> (1) the statutory criteria;
>
> (2) application of CERCLA §107(q) to current and former owners of property;
>
> (3) the relationship between CERCLA § 107(q) and the EPA's _Residential Homeowner Policy_ and _Contaminated Aquifers Policy_; and
>
> (4) discretionary mechanisms the EPA may use to address remaining liability concerns of contiguous property owners.

In 2009, the EPA issued the _Model CERCLA Section 107(q)(3) Contiguous Property Owner Assurance Letter_ in accordance with the 2004 enforcement discretion guidance mentioned above to be used under specified circumstances. Because CERCLA §107 (q) is self-implementing, the EPA anticipates that use of such letters will be limited.

3. Third Party Defense and Innocent Landowners

Entities that acquire property and have no knowledge of the contamination at the time of purchase may be eligible for CERCLA's third party defense or innocent landowner defense, in addition to the BFPP defense.

i.   Third Party Defense

CERCLA § 107(b) includes the following defenses to liability if a person can show, by a preponderance of the evidence, that the contamination was solely caused by:

- An act of God (CERCLA § 107(b)(1));

- An act of war (CERCLA § 107(b)(2)); or

- The act or omission of a third party (CERCLA § 107(b)(3)).

To invoke CERCLA's § 107(b)(3) third party defense, the third party's act or omission must not occur "in connection with a contractual relationship." Moreover, an entity asserting the CERCLA § 107(b)(3) defense must show that: (a) it exercised due care with respect to the contamination; and (b) it took precautions against the third party's foreseeable acts or omissions and the consequences that could foreseeably result from such acts or omissions.

ii.   Innocent Landowners

The Superfund Amendments and Reauthorization Act of 1986 (Public Law 96-510) expanded the third-party defense by creating innocent landowner exclusions to the definition of a "contractual relationship." Previously, the deed transferring title between a PRP and the new landowner was a "contractual relationship" that prevented the new landowner from raising the traditional CERCLA § 107(b)(3) third party defense. To promote redevelopment and provide more certainty, Congress created the "innocent landowner defense," which requires an entity to meet the criteria set forth in CERCLA § 101(35) in addition to the requirements of CERCLA § 107(b)(3). CERCLA § 101(35)(A) distinguishes among three types of innocent landowners:

- Purchasers who acquire property without knowledge of contamination and who have no reason to know about the contamination, CERCLA § 101(35) (A)(i);

- Governments "which acquired the facility by escheat, or through any other involuntary transfers or acquisition, or through the exercise of eminent domain authority by purchase or condemnation," CERCLA § 101(35)(A)(ii); and

- Inheritors of contaminated property, CERCLA § 101(35)(A)(ii).

For all three types of landowners, the facility must be acquired after the disposal or placement of the hazardous substances on, in, or at the facility. Further, a set of continuing obligations similar to what is required of BFPPs also applies. CERCLA § 101 (35)(A).

For purchasers who acquire property without knowledge of contamination after 2002, an owner must have conducted AAI before purchase and complied with other pre- and post-purchase requirements. The Brownfields Amendments also elaborated on the AAI requirement. See the "All Appropriate Inquiries" text box.

4.   Common Elements Guidance

In 2003, the EPA issued its "Common Elements" guidance for the three property owner classes -- bona fide prospective purchaser (BFPP), contiguous property owner, and innocent landowner -- added to CERCLA in 2002. See *Interim Guidance Regarding Criteria Landowners Must Meet in Order to Qualify for Bona Fide Prospective Purchaser, Contiguous Property Owner, or Innocent Landowner Limitations on CERCLA Liability ("Common Elements")*. CERCLA identifies threshold criteria and ongoing obligations that these types of landowners must meet to obtain the liability protections afforded by the statute. Many of these obligations are overlapping - thus the shorthand name "Common Elements" for the guidance. The guidance was accompanied by the *"Common Elements" Guidance Reference Sheet*, which highlights the significant points of the guidance.

The Common Elements guidance first discusses the threshold criteria BFPPs, contiguous property owners, and innocent landowners must meet to assert these liability protections. The first requirement is that the landowner must perform all appropriate inquiries (AAI) before purchasing the property. CERCLA §§ 101(40)(B), 107(q)(1)(A)(viii), 101(35)(A)(i), and (B)(i).

ALL APPROPRIATE INQUIRIES

BFPPs, contiguous property owners, and innocent landowners must all undertake "all appropriate inquiries" (AAI) under CERCLA § 101(35)(B) before acquiring property to obtain liability protection. CERCLA § 101(35)(B) required the EPA to publish a regulation to "establish standards and practices for the purpose of satisfying the requirement to carry out [AAI] . . . ." The EPA's All Appropriate Inquiries Rule (AAI Rule), 40 C.F.R. Part 312 (1996), establishes those requirements. Parties affected by the AAI Rule are those purchasing commercial or industrial real estate who wish to take advantage of CERCLA's landowner liability protections and those persons conducting a site characterization or assessment with funds provided by certain federal brownfields grants.

Second, the BFPP and contiguous property owner protections require that the purchaser not be "affiliated" with a liable party, (CERCLA §§ 101(40)(H), 107(q)(1)(A)(ii)). For the innocent landowner defense, the act or omission that caused the release or threat of release of hazardous substances and the resulting damages must have been caused by a third party with whom the purchaser does not have an employment, agency, or contractual relationship. CERCLA §§ 107(b)(3), 101(35)(A).

AFFILIATION

The BFPP and contiguous property owner liability protections require that the purchaser or owner of the property at issue not be "affiliated" with a person who is potentially liable at that property. For both liability protections, "affiliation" includes a familial, contractual, financial, or corporate relationship. The affiliation language is found in CERCLA § 101(40) for those seeking liability protection as a BFPP, while the affiliation language for a contiguous property owner is found in CERCLA § 107(q)(1)(A). The contiguous property owner affiliation language differs from the BFPP affiliation language in that there is no exception for relationships created by the instruments by which title to the facility is conveyed or financed. Except for this difference, the affiliation language in the BFPP and contiguous property owner provisions is identical.

In 2011, the EPA issued *Enforcement Discretion Guidance Regarding the Affiliation Language of CERCLA's Bona Fide Prospective and Contiguous Property Owner Liability Protections* on how it intends to apply the affiliation language in the BFPP and contiguous property owner liability protections to individual property owners. This memorandum is meant to provide assistance to EPA regional attorneys in evaluating whether specific circumstances run afoul of the "no affiliation" clauses in CERCLA. To that end, the memorandum is divided into two sections: the first addresses general guidance regarding the statutory language, while the second addresses the three situations in which the EPA will exercise its enforcement discretion for non-site related relationships, post-acquisition relationships, and tenants. The guidance uses questions and answers and more specific examples to explain the statutory language and the EPA's intention for the use of enforcement discretion.

Third, the Common Elements guidance discusses the common ongoing obligations for each type of landowner liability protection, identified as follows:

- Complying with land use restrictions and not impeding the effectiveness or integrity of institutional controls;

- Taking "reasonable steps to prevent releases" with respect to hazardous substances affecting a landowner's property;

- Providing cooperation, assistance, and access to the property;

- Complying with information requests and subpoenas; and

- Providing legally required notices.

Finally, the guidance includes three documents:

(1) A chart laying out the common statutory obligations;

(2) A questions and answers document pertaining to the "reasonable steps" criteria; and

(3) A model comfort/status letter for providing site-specific suggestions as to reasonable steps.

Prospective purchasers or owners of contaminated property may want to look to the Common Elements guidance to understand the different liability protections that may be available and their requirements.

MacGillis & Gibbs Co./Bell Lumber & Pole Co. – New Brighton, Minnesota

The 68-acre MacGillis & Gibbs Co./Bell Lumber & Pole Co. Superfund site consists of two adjoining wood preserving facility properties in New Brighton, Minnesota. Since the mid-1980s, the City had been laying the groundwork necessary to redevelop the 25-acre MacGillis & Gibbs property. In 1997, the City, along with state and federal agencies, successfully negotiated a PPA to resolve the City's liability concerns about acquiring the property. Today, the site redevelopment includes manufacturing and distribution businesses, as well as over 70,000 square feet of commercial office space, a range of retail shops and restaurants, legal and medical services, a post office, and a 120-unit condominium development.

B.   State Response Programs

1.   Voluntary Cleanup Programs

State response programs play a significant role in assessing and cleaning up brownfield sites. Voluntary cleanup programs (VCPs) are typically programs authorized by state statutes to address brownfields and other lower-risk sites. Additional information on State VCPs can be found on the EPA's State and Tribal Response Programs Agreements website.

The EPA has historically supported the use of VCPs and continues to provide grant funding to establish and enhance VCPs. The EPA also continues to provide general enforcement assurances to individual states to encourage the assessment and cleanup of sites addressed under VCP oversight. This approach to VCPs was codified in 2002 as CERCLA § 128:

- CERCLA § 128(a) addresses grant funding and memoranda of agreement (MOAs) for state response programs (i.e., VCPs);

- CERCLA § 128(b) addresses the "enforcement bar," which limits EPA enforcement actions under CERCLA §§ 106(a) and 107(a) at "eligible response sites" addressed in compliance with state response programs that specifically govern cleanups to protect human health and the environment; and

- CERCLA § 128(b)(1)(C) addresses the establishment and maintenance of a public record by a state to document the cleanup and potential use restrictions of sites addressed by a VCP.

2.   Memorandum of Agreement

Since 1995, the EPA has encouraged the use of VCPs at lower-risk sites by entering into non-binding memoranda of agreement (MOAs) with interested states based on a review of the state VCP's capabilities. MOAs can be valuable mechanisms to support and strengthen efforts to achieve protective cleanups under VCP oversight. The purpose of the MOAs is to foster more effective and efficient working relationships between the EPA and individual states regarding the use of their VCPs. Specifically, MOAs define the EPA and state roles and responsibilities and provide the EPA's recognition of the state's capabilities. MOAs typically include a general statement of the EPA's enforcement intentions regarding certain sites cleaned up under the oversight of a VCP.

A number of states are also using their VCPs to address facilities subject to RCRA corrective action. As a result, the EPA and several states have expanded upon the CERCLA VCP MOA concept to address some facilities subject to RCRA corrective action. Those agreements are commonly known as RCRA Memoranda of Understanding (MOUs). The EPA has also entered into a few MOAs that address multiple cleanup programs.

3.   Eligible Response Sites and the Enforcement Bar

Under CERCLA an "eligible response site" (CERCLA § 101(41)) is a site at which the EPA may not take an enforcement action under CERCLA §§ 106 or 107 because it is already being cleaned up under a state response program. This prohibition on federal enforcement is commonly known as the enforcement bar. CERCLA § 128 (b). Eligible sites also may be eligible for deferral from listing on the National Priorities List (NPL) in certain circumstances. CERCLA § 105(h). If an EPA region determines that a site is not an "eligible response site," that site will not be subject to the deferral provisions in CERCLA § 105(h) and the limitations on the EPA's enforcement and cost recovery authorities under CERCLA § 128(b). For more information on eligible response sites, see the EPA's 2003 guidance _Regional Determinations Regarding Which Sites Are Not "Eligible Response Sites."_

C.   Local Government Liability Protections

1.   Involuntary Acquisition

CERCLA provides that a unit of state or local government will not be considered an owner or operator of contaminated property (and thus will be exempt from potential CERCLA liability as a PRP) if the state or local government acquired ownership or control involuntarily. This provision includes a non-exhaustive list of examples of involuntary acquisitions, including obtaining property through bankruptcy, tax delinquency, abandonment, or "other circumstances in which the government entity involuntarily acquires title by virtue of its function as a sovereign." CERCLA § 101(20)(D). It is important to note that this exclusion will not apply to any state or local government that caused or contributed to the release or threatened release of a hazardous substance from a facility.

MEANING OF "INVOLUNTARY ACQUISITION"

In the 1995 policy _Municipal Immunity from CERCLA Liability for Property Acquired through Involuntary State Action_, the EPA stated that an involuntary acquisition or transfer includes one "in which the government's interest in, and ultimate ownership of, a specific asset exists only because the conduct of a non-governmental party… gives rise to a statutory or common law right to property on behalf of the government." The EPA acknowledges that tax foreclosure and other acquisitions by government entities often require some affirmative or volitional act by the local government. Therefore, a government entity does not have to be completely passive during the acquisition in order for the acquisition of property to be considered "involuntary" under CERCLA. Instead, the EPA considers an acquisition to be "involuntary" if the government's interest in, and ultimate ownership of, the property exists only because the actions of a non-governmental party give rise to the government's legal right to control or take title to the property.

CERCLA § 101(35)(A)(ii) also discusses involuntary acquisitions in the context of the innocent landowner defense pursuant to CERCLA § 101(35)(A). Please see Section III.A.3.ii for further detail.

The EPA has a webpage dedicated to state and local government activities and liability protections, which includes a 2011 fact sheet titled *CERCLA Liability and Local Government Acquisition and Other Activities* and a workbook called *Process for Risk Evaluation, Property Analysis and Reuse Decisions for Local Governments Considering the Reuse of Contaminated Properties (PDF)* (210 pp).

2. Emergency Response

Local units of government, especially fire, health, and public safety departments, are often the first responders to emergencies and dangerous situations at contaminated properties in their communities. To prevent interference with these activities, Congress included the emergency response exemption in CERCLA § 107(d)(2). Under this provision, state or local governments will not be liable for "costs or damages as a result of actions taken in response to an emergency created by a release or threatened release of a hazardous substance." To qualify, the state or local government must not own the property and must not act in a grossly negligent manner or intentionally engage in misconduct. Further, the EPA may reimburse local governments up to $25,000 for the costs of temporary measures under CERCLA § 123.

3. Land Banks

An increasing number of states and municipalities are passing legislation that authorizes land banks. Enabled by state legislation and enacted by local ordinances, a land bank is a governmental entity or nonprofit that acquires, holds, leases, and/or manages vacant, abandoned, and tax delinquent properties. They are tasked with returning such properties to productive use. Land banks can allow local governments to overcome redevelopment barriers that prevent the conversion of underutilized land to higher uses. They can also facilitate land reuse while advancing public policy goals such as providing affordable housing; stabilizing neighborhoods; developing open space; revitalizing brownfields; planning for smart growth; and reducing crime, potential fire hazards, and urban blight.

STATES WITH LAND BANK LEGISLATION

Michigan	Kentucky
New York	Maryland
Ohio	Missouri
Georgia	Tennessee
Indiana	Pennsylvania
Texas	

Although the responsibilities of land banks will vary according to state law and the authorizing legislation, common responsibilities and authorities of a land bank include taking inventory of vacant and abandoned properties, acquiring, managing, and selling properties, and waiving delinquent taxes.

While many land bank properties may not be contaminated, it is important to be aware of the potential for contamination. Purchasers of property from a land bank may want to assess whether there is an applicable CERCLA exemption, affirmative defense, or liability protection. These concerns also apply in the local government involuntary acquisition context. Whether a local government that acquires a land bank property will qualify under the involuntary acquisition exemption, BFPP liability protection, or third party defense is determined on a case-by-case basis.

U.S. Environmental Protection Agency
Office of Site Remediation Enforcement

D.   Lender Liability Protections

1.   CERCLA Secured Creditor Exemption

Under CERCLA's secured creditor exemption, a lender is not an "owner or operator" under CERCLA if, "without participating in the management" of a vessel or facility, it holds indicia of ownership primarily to protect its security interest. CERCLA §§ 101(20)(E)-(G). CERCLA § 101(20)(E) defines key terms and lists activities that a lender may undertake without forfeiting the exemption. Additional information is available in the "Participation in Management" text box below. The EPA also has issued enforcement guidance to address these statutory provisions. *See Policy on Interpreting CERCLA Provisions Addressing Lenders and Involuntary Acquisitions by Government Entities*.

"PARTICIPATION IN MANAGEMENT"

A lender "participates in management" (and will not qualify for the exemption) if the lender:

- Exercises decisionmaking control over environmental compliance related to the facility and, in doing so, undertakes responsibility for hazardous substance handling or disposal practices;
- Exercises control at a level similar to that of a manager of the facility and, in doing so, assumes or manifests responsibility with respect to day-to-day decision making with respect to environmental compliance; or
- Exercises all, or substantially all, of the operational (as opposed to financial or administrative) functions of the facility other than environmental compliance.

The term "participate in management" does not include certain activities such as when the lender:

- Inspects the facility;
- Requires a response action or other lawful means to address a release or threatened release;
- Conducts a response action under CERCLA § 107(d)(1) or under the direction of the EPA;
- Provides financial or other advice in an effort to prevent or cure default; or
- Restructures or renegotiates the terms of the security interest provided the actions do not rise to the level of participating in management.

After foreclosure, a lender who did not participate in management before foreclosure is not an "owner or operator" if the lender:

- Sells, releases (in the case of a lease finance transaction), or liquidates the facility;
- Maintains business activities or winds up operations;
- Undertakes an emergency response or action under the direction of the EPA; or
- Takes any other measure to preserve, protect, or prepare the facility for sale or disposition provided the lender seeks to divest itself of the facility at the earliest practicable, commercially reasonable time, on commercially reasonable terms. The EPA considers this test to be met if the lender, within 12 months of foreclosure, lists the property with a broker or advertises it for sale in an appropriate publication.

2. Underground Storage Tank Lender Liability Protection

Local communities often struggle with what to do about polluted, abandoned gas stations and other petroleum-contaminated properties, generally referred to as petroleum brownfields. Often, citizens and businesses shy away from the reuse potential of these properties, fearing the potential liability of environmental contamination under the underground storage tank (UST) provisions of RCRA. RCRA § 9003(h)(9), which codified EPA's UST Lender Liability Rule (40 C.F.R. § 280.200 et seq.), addresses the fear of potential lender liability to encourage the reuse of abandoned gas station sites.

Certain classes of "owner" and "operator" (i.e., holders of security interests as described in the rule) are exempt from RCRA regulatory requirements such as corrective action, technical requirements, and financial responsibility, provided that specified criteria are met. Security interest holders are required to empty tanks acquired through foreclosure, thus preventing future releases. By allowing security interest holders to market their foreclosed properties without incurring RCRA liability, gas stations are reused when they otherwise may have been abandoned.

E. Residential Property Owners

In 1991, the EPA issued the *Policy Towards Owners of Residential Properties at Superfund Sites*. The goal of this enforcement discretion policy is to relieve residential owners of the fear that they might be subject to an enforcement action involving contaminated property, even though they had not caused the contamination on the property.

Under this policy, residential property is defined as "single family residences of one-to-four dwelling units. . . ." Further, this policy deems irrelevant a residential owner's knowledge of contamination. The residential owner policy applies to residents as well as their lessees, so long as the activities the resident takes on the property are consistent with the policy. The policy also applies to residential owners who acquire property through purchase, foreclosure, gift, inheritance, or other form of acquisition, as long as the activities the resident undertakes on the property after acquisition are consistent with the policy.

Residential property owners who purchase contaminated property after January 1, 2002, may also take advantage of the statutory BFPP protection. The Brownfields Amendments addressed residential property owners by clarifying the type of pre-purchase investigation (i.e., AAI) that a residential property owner must conduct to obtain BFPP status. Specifically, an inspection and title search that reveal no basis for further investigation will qualify as all appropriate inquiry for a residential purchaser. CERCLA § 101(40)(B) (iii).

CRITERIA FOR RESIDENTIAL
PROPERTY OWNERS UNDER EPA POLICY

An owner of residential property located on a CERCLA site may be protected from liability if the owner:

- Has not engaged and does not engage in activities that lead to a release or threat of release of hazardous substances, resulting in the EPA taking a response action at the site;
- Cooperates fully with the EPA by providing access and information when requested and does not interfere with the activities that either the EPA or a state is taking to implement a CERCLA response action;
- Does not improve the property in a manner inconsistent with residential use; and
- Complies with institutional controls (e.g., property use restrictions) that may be placed on the residential property as part of the EPA's response action.

IV. Site-Specific EPA Tools to Address Cleanup Status, Liability Concerns, and/or Perceived Stigma

A. Comfort/Status Letters

Comfort/status letters provide a prospective purchaser with the information the EPA has about a particular property and the EPA's intentions with respect to the property as of the date of the letter. The "comfort" comes from a greater understanding of what the EPA knows about the property and what its intentions are with respect to any response activities. Comfort/status letters are not "no action" assurances; that is, they are not assurances by the EPA that it will not take an enforcement action at a particular site in the future. They are intended for use in limited circumstances and subject to the availability of Agency resources.

1. Superfund Comfort/Status Letters

In 1996, the EPA issued its *Policy on the Issuance of Comfort/Status Letters*, which included models for use by regions when developing site-specific letters. The letters provide a party with relevant releasable information the EPA has pertaining to a particular piece of property, what that information means, and the status of any ongoing, completed or planned federal Superfund action at the property. Comfort/status letters may be considered when they may facilitate the cleanup and redevelopment of brownfields, where there is a realistic perception or probability of incurring Superfund liability, and where there is no other mechanism available to adequately address a party's concerns.

> **EVALUATION CRITERIA FOR SUPERFUND COMFORT/STATUS LETTERS**
>
> The EPA may issue a comfort letter upon request if:
>
> - The letter may facilitate cleanup and redevelopment of potentially contaminated property;
> - There is a realistic perception or probability of incurring CERCLA liability; and
> - There is no other mechanism available to adequately address the party's concerns.

2. Reasonable Steps Comfort/Status Letters

The EPA has the discretion, in appropriate circumstances, to provide a BFPP (see Section III.A.1), contiguous property owner (see Section III.A.2.ii), or innocent landowner (see Section III.A.3.ii) with a comfort/status letter addressing what "reasonable steps" a landowner could take at a particular site to meet its continuing obligations with respect to hazardous substances found at the property. When issuing this type of letter, the EPA makes an assessment of the actions proposed by the landowner and, based on site-specific factors and environmental concerns, determines any potential incompatibilities between the proposed site activities and the EPA's response actions. The EPA also suggests what steps might be appropriate for the landowner to take with respect to the planned or completed response action. This letter does not provide a release from CERCLA liability, but only provides information with respect to reasonable steps based on the available information and the nature and extent of contamination known to the EPA at the time the letter is issued. If additional information regarding the nature and extent of hazardous substance contamination at the site becomes available, additional actions may be necessary to satisfy the reasonable steps requirement.

3. Renewable Energy Comfort/Status Letters

In 2012, the EPA issued three new model Superfund comfort/status letters specifically intended for lessees involved in renewable energy development on contaminated property. The letters are intended to provide the lessee with information the EPA currently has about the property and applicable Agency policies to help the lessee make informed decisions as they move forward with renewable energy development on their property. The letters were released with the *Revised Enforcement Guidance Regarding the Treatment of Tenants Under the CERCLA Bona Fide Prospective Purchaser Provision*.

4. RCRA Comfort/Status Letters

RCRA treatment, storage, and disposal facilities (TSDF) present unique challenges in terms of cleanup and reuse, but may also provide opportunities for revitalization. Recognizing that situations often exist at RCRA facilities analogous to those at Superfund sites, the EPA developed guidance for issuing comfort/status letters for RCRA TSD facilities. The EPA further explained the proper use of RCRA comfort/status letters in its guidance *Prospective Purchaser Agreements and Other Tools to Facilitate Cleanup and Reuse of RCRA Sites*. In *Comfort/Status Letters for RCRA Brownfield Properties*, the EPA indicated that it would limit the use of such letters to those situations that could facilitate the cleanup and reuse of brownfields, where there was a realistic perception or probability of the EPA initiating a RCRA cleanup action, and where there was no other mechanism to adequately address the party's concern.

5. Comfort/Status Letters for Federally Owned Properties

The EPA may issue a comfort/status letter to address various issues concerning perceived NPL stigma and CERCLA liability involved with a military property. In 1996, the EPA updated its *Model Comfort Letter Clarifying NPL Listing, Uncontaminated Parcel Identifications, and CERCLA Liability Issues Involving Transfers of Federally Owned Property*. This type of comfort/status letter may include a determination that a remedy is operating properly and successfully.

The model letter also describes certain CERCLA provisions applicable to a federal agency before transferring any property on which hazardous substances have been stored for a year or more, or are known to have been released or disposed of. The EPA's Federal Facilities Restoration and Reuse Office webpage further explains efforts to clean up, transfer, and reuse federal facilities.

B. Agreements

The use of an agreement may be appropriate for certain sites to address liability concerns to encourage reuse or revitalization.

1. Bona Fide Prospective Purchaser Work Agreements

The activities of most BFPPs will not require liability protection beyond what is provided by the self-implementing BFPP protection in CERCLA. However, if a BFPP wants to perform cleanup work at a contaminated site of federal interest that exceeds the BFPP reasonable steps requirement, a work agreement may be used to address potential liability concerns.

In 2006, the EPA and DOJ jointly issued the *CERCLA Model Agreement and Order on Consent for Removal Action by a Bona Fide Prospective Purchaser* for use as a removal work agreement with a BFPP at a site of federal interest. In particular, the removal work to be performed under the agreement must be of greater scope and magnitude than the "reasonable steps" with respect to the hazardous substances at the property that must be performed by BFPPs if they are to maintain their protected status under the statute. The model agreement provides a covenant not to sue for "existing contamination" and requires the person performing the removal work to reimburse the EPA's oversight costs. Contribution protection and a release and waiver of any windfall lien are also provided.

2.   **Prospective Purchaser Agreements and Prospective Lessee Agreements**

Before the BFPP liability protection was available, the EPA entered into Prospective Purchasers Agreements (PPAs) and Prospective Lessee Agreements (PLAs) with a party facing potential CERCLA liability to provide the party with liability relief in exchange for payment and/or cleanup work. PPAs and PLAs are available for CERCLA and RCRA sites.

Between 1989 and 2006, the EPA issued the following policies that address the use of PPAs and PLAs:

- *Guidance on Landowner Liability under Section 107(a)(1) of CERCLA, De Minimis Settlements under Section 122(g)(1)(B) of CERCLA, and Settlements with Prospective Purchasers of Contaminated Property*. Models attached to the 1989 guidance are for settlements with *de minimis* landowners under § 122(g)(1)(B).

- *Guidance on Agreements with Prospective Purchasers of Contaminated Property*.

- *Expediting Requests for Prospective Purchaser Agreements*.

- *Support of Regional Efforts to Negotiate Prospective Purchaser Agreements (PPAs) at Superfund Sites and Clarification of PPA Guidance*.

- *Memorandum on Prospective Purchaser Agreements and Other Tools to Facilitate Cleanup and Reuse of RCRA Sites*.

- *Final Guidance on Completion of Corrective Action Activities at RCRA Facilities (PDF)* (8 pp.).

- *Bona Fide Prospective Purchasers and the New Amendments to CERCLA*.

- *Issuance of CERCLA Model Agreement and Order on Consent for Removal Action by a Bona Fide Prospective Purchaser*.

These documents discuss the interplay between the statutory BFPP protection and the EPA's continued use of PPAs. The EPA stated that, in most circumstances, where a party meets the BFPP requirements, PPAs will no longer be needed to provide liability relief under CERCLA as a present owner.

There are, however, limited circumstances under which the EPA will continue to consider entering into a PPA, such as when:

- Significant environmental benefits will be derived from the project in terms of cleanup;

- The facility is currently involved in CERCLA litigation such that there is a very real possibility that a party who buys the facility would be sued by a third party; and

- There are unique, site-specific circumstances not otherwise addressed and the PPA will serve a significant public interest.

DIFFERENCES BETWEEN BFPP LIABILITY PROTECTION AND PPAS

	BFPP	PPAs
Method of Execution	Self-Implementing	Negotiation and EPA and DOJ approval
Timing	Obtained when purchaser meets threshold and maintains statutory requirements	Obtained after federal government approves PPA terms
Transaction Costs	Lower transaction costs	Higher transaction costs

3.   Windfall Lien Resolution Agreements

In *Interim Enforcement Discretion Policy Concerning "Windfall Liens" Under Section 107(r) of CERCLA*, the EPA anticipates that there may be situations where a site has a windfall lien (for more on windfall liens, see Section III.A.1) and a BFPP wants to satisfy any existing or potential windfall lien before or close to the time of acquisition. Congress specifically provided the EPA with the authority to resolve windfall liens in CERCLA § 107(r)(2). The EPA and DOJ have developed a model agreement to facilitate resolution of windfall liens as an attachment to the windfall liens guidance.

4.   Contiguous Property Owner Assurance Letters and Settlements

The Brownfields Amendments provide CERCLA liability protection for contiguous property owners (CPOs). Some landowners, however, continue to have liability concerns especially where the EPA has conducted a response action on the neighboring contaminated property or the contiguous property owner's property. In such cases, the EPA has the discretion to offer assurance that no enforcement action will be brought against a contiguous property owner for contamination resulting from a neighbor's actions. Alternatively, the EPA may enter into a

U.S. Environmental Protection Agency
Office of Site Remediation Enforcement

settlement agreement with the contiguous property owner, providing the contiguous property owner with cost recovery or contribution protection from PRPs at the site. The EPA's *Interim Enforcement Discretion Guidance Regarding Contiguous Property Owners* and *Model CERCLA Section 107(q)(3) Contiguous Property Owner Assurance Letter* provide guidance on when such an assurance letter or agreement is appropriate.

Former Spellman Engineering Site – Orlando, Florida

Working relationships and innovative settlement agreements led to the cleanup of the Former Spellman Engineering site and reuse of the adjacent Lake Highland property in Orlando, Florida. In 2008, the EPA and the City of Orlando signed the nation's first CPO agreement, in which the City agreed to voluntarily implement the site's estimated $12.9 million remedy. Lake Highland Preparatory School (LHPS) also

worked with the City to finalize the project's Sale and Purchase agreement and with the City, the EPA and Florida Department of Environmental Protection to finalize BFPP and Brownfield Site Rehabilitation agreements that addressed potential liability concerns and facilitated the property's reuse. LHPS has been able to reuse 18 acres of the Lake Highland property, providing much-needed sports fields and parking. The City and the Orlando Utilities Commission are exploring opportunities for remaining portions of the property to encourage mixed-use redevelopment near public transit facilities.

C. Other Tools

1. Ready for Reuse Determinations

When all or a portion of a Superfund site is protective for specified uses, the EPA has the discretion to issue a Ready for Reuse (RfR) Determination. RfR Determinations are intended to facilitate reuse and provide helpful information to the real estate marketplace about the environmental status of the Superfund site.

RfR Determinations are technical rather than legal and explain the nature and extent of contamination. Before the EPA created the RfR Determination, potential users often had to seek out information about a site's environmental condition from many different sources, and the information that was available was often expressed in technical terms difficult for the marketplace to interpret. This meant that many sites able to accommodate certain types of uses were needlessly difficult to market. With the creation of the RfR Determination, potential users and the real estate marketplace have an affirmative statement written in plain English and accompanied by supporting decision documentation that a site identified as ready for reuse will remain protective of the remedy as long as all required response conditions and use limitations identified in the site's response decision documents and land title documents continue to be met. For more information, please see the EPA's *Guidance for Preparing Superfund Ready for Reuse Determinations*.

Arlington Blending and Packaging –Arlington, Tennessee

From 1971 to 1978, Arlington Blending and Packaging operated a pesticide processing and packaging facility at what is now a Superfund site in Arlington, Tennessee. The EPA provided the Town of Arlington with a comfort letter and a Ready for Reuse (RfR) determination, which assured the Town that the site had been remediated to a standard that would permit recreational reuse. In November 2006, the collaborative efforts of the Arlington community and the EPA came to fruition as the new Mary Alice Park officially opened to the public with a ribbon-cutting ceremony.

2.   **National Priorities List Deletions**

Under certain conditions, the EPA may delete or recategorize a property or portion of a property from the NPL. States play a key role in NPL deletions. Before developing a notice of intent to delete, the EPA must consult with the state. In consultation with the state, the EPA must consider:

- Whether responsible parties or other parties have taken all appropriate response actions that are required;

- Whether no further response actions are required; and

- Whether the remedial investigation has shown that the release poses no significant threat to public health or the environment and taking of remedial measures is, therefore, not appropriate.

Sites may not be deleted from the NPL without state concurrence and publication of a proposed deletion in the Federal Register. It is important to note that deletion or partial deletion of a site from the NPL does not itself create, alter, or remove any legal rights or obligations.

PRIVATE PARTY TOOLS

Various private tools can be used to manage environmental liability risks associated with brownfields and other properties. These tools may include:

- Indemnification Provisions -These are private contractual mechanisms in which one party promises to cover the costs of liability of another party. Indemnification provisions provide prospective buyers, lenders, insurers, and developers with a means of assigning responsibility among themselves for cleanup costs, and encourage negotiations among private parties without government involvement.
- Environmental Insurance Policies -The insurance industry offers products intended to allocate and minimize liability exposures among parties involved in brownfields redevelopment. These products include cost cap, pollution legal liability, and secured creditor policies. Insurance products may serve as a tool to manage environmental liability risks, but many factors affect their utility including the types of coverage available, the dollar limits on claims, the policy time limits, site assessment requirements, and the cost of available products. Parties involved in brownfields redevelopment considering environmental insurance should retain the assistance of skilled brokers and lawyers to help select appropriate coverage.

U.S. Environmental Protection Agency
Office of Site Remediation Enforcement

V. Other Considerations for Entities Seeking to Clean Up, Reuse, and Revitalize Contaminated Property

A. Long-Term Stewardship

Long-term stewardship generally refers to the activities and processes used to control and manage residual contamination, limit inappropriate exposures, control land and resource uses, and ensure the continued protectiveness of "engineered" controls and effectiveness of "institutional" controls at sites. Long-term stewardship activities take on greater importance with the increased demand for the reuse of properties, especially properties where some contamination remains.

Physical or "engineered" controls are the engineered physical barriers or structures designed to monitor and prevent or limit exposure to the contamination at a site. Certain engineered cleanups will involve ongoing operations and maintenance (O&M), monitoring, evaluation, periodic repairs, and sometimes replacement of remedy components.

"Institutional" controls (ICs) are non-engineered instruments, such as administrative and/or legal mechanisms, intended to minimize the potential for human exposure to contamination by limiting land or resource use at a site. Institutional controls may be used to supplement engineering controls and also must be implemented, monitored, and evaluated for effectiveness as long as the risks at a site are present.

EXAMPLES OF ENGINEERED CONTROLS	EXAMPLES OF INSTITUTIONAL CONTROLS
• Landfill soil caps	• Government Controls -- Permits, Zoning
• Impermeable liners	• Informational Devices -- Notices, Advisories, Warnings, Signs, Deed Notices
• Other containment covers	
• Underground slurry walls	• Proprietary Controls -- Easements, Restrictive Covenants
• Fences	
• Bioremediation	• Enforcement Mechanisms -- Administrative Orders, Cleanup Agreements
• Ground water pump-and-treat and monitoring systems	

The EPA has published a number of useful guidance documents on ICs. In 2005, to further explain the requirements of institutional controls, the EPA published a guidance document titled _Institutional Controls: A Citizen's Guide to Understanding Institutional Controls at Superfund, Brownfields, Federal Facilities, Underground Storage Tanks, and Resource Conservation and Recovery Act Cleanups_.

In 2012, the EPA also published two cross-program guidance documents addressing the entire lifecycle of ICs, titled _Institutional Controls: A Guide to Planning, Implementing, Maintaining, and Enforcing Institutional Controls at Contaminated Sites (PIME)_ and _Institutional Controls: A Guide to Preparing Institutional Control Implementation and Assurance Plans at Contaminated Sites (ICIAP)_.

The PIME guidance identifies and addresses many of the common issues that may be encountered when using ICs pursuant to several cleanup programs. It also provides an overview of the EPA's policy regarding the roles and responsibilities of stakeholders involved in various aspects of the IC life cycle.

The ICIAP guidance provides the EPA regions with a template for developing IC plans at contaminated sites where the response action includes ICs. An ICIAP is a document designed to systematically establish and document the activities associated with implementing and ensuring the long-term stewardship of ICs, and specify the persons and/or entities that will be responsible for conducting these activities.

The EPA, the states, and local governments have increased their knowledge about the long-term requirements needed to reuse and revitalize contaminated sites. The cleanup remedies for contaminated sites and properties often require the management and oversight of on-site waste materials and contaminated environmental media for long periods of time. The EPA and its regulatory partners implement (or ensure that responsible parties implement) long-term stewardship activities after remedy construction for as long as those activities are needed to help ensure protectiveness. Long-term stewardship can last years, decades, or in some cases, even longer. Long-term stewardship may involve ongoing coordination and communication among numerous stakeholders, each with different responsibilities, capabilities, and information needs.

Even though the various cleanup programs have different authorities, there are similarities to address the long-term stewardship efforts. For example, under Superfund, long-term stewardship activities are performed as part of the O&M of a remedy. Responsibility for O&M depends upon whether the cleanup was conducted by a potentially responsible party (PRP), including at federal facilities, or whether the EPA funded the cleanup. Under the RCRA program, the facility owner is responsible for the O&M.

Under the brownfields program, the EPA provides cleanup grants to state and local governments and non-profit organizations to carry out cleanup activities, including IC activities.

Midvale Slag – Midvale, Utah

The potential redevelopment of the 446-acre Midvale Slag site presented a vital opportunity for Midvale City, Utah, the local citizens and the site owner. Thanks to a cleanup that integrated future use considerations, the EPA's issuance of an RfR Determination and the use of special account resources to fund a local government expert to implement and oversee institutional controls, the site safely supports a thriving mixed-use development envisioned by the community. The EPA and Midvale City collaborated to develop two Institutional Control Process Plans and, to implement and oversee them, Midvale City's Department of Community and Economic Development created a full-time position to assist the community. The outcomes are striking: approximately 800 jobs, $1.8 million in annual property tax revenues and a $145 million increase in the value of the site property. With more than 2,500 residential units planned and construction underway, families have moved into new on-site condominiums and single-family homes.

Pursuant to the UST program requirements, when a release has been detected or discovered at an UST, the UST owner/operator must perform corrective action to clean up any contamination caused by the release. Under cooperative agreements between the EPA and the states, states are largely responsible for overseeing corrective actions in connection with USTs, including long-term stewardship. The EPA is generally responsible for overseeing the corrective actions, including long-term stewardship activities on tribal lands.

U.S. Environmental Protection Agency
Office of Site Remediation Enforcement

B.   Guiding Principles of the EPA's Enforcement Program

The EPA's enforcement program is guided in the development of policy and guidance documents not only by enforcement principles such as "polluter pays" and "enforcement first," but also by the following principles that have been established to carry out the EPA's mission.

1.   Supplemental Environmental Projects

In certain circumstances, supplemental environmental projects (SEPs) may play a role in revitalizing contaminated sites. SEPs are not developed, funded, or managed by the EPA. Rather, they are environmentally beneficial projects undertaken by a defendant or respondent in settlement of an environmental enforcement action. SEPs are activities that go beyond what is required for compliance and that the violator is not otherwise legally required to perform. The EPA's *Issuance of Final Supplemental Environmental Projects Policy* describes when and how a SEP may be included as part of an enforcement settlement. Although not appropriate for every enforcement settlement, where a violator is willing and the conditions of the SEP Policy are met, SEPs may help address environmental concerns related to the violations at issue in the enforcement action.

As stated in the 2006 *Brownfield Sites and Supplemental Environmental Projects* fact sheet, SEPs that require assessment and/or cleanup of brownfield sites cannot be included in settlements because appropriations law prohibits the Agency from including SEPs to perform activities that Congress has already funded through the EPA. Congress provides funds for assessment and cleanup activities to the EPA's brownfields program. In an appropriate enforcement settlement, however, SEPs that complement brownfield site assessment or cleanup activities may be included in the settlement. Examples of such SEPs are green building projects, projects that call for the violator to provide energy-efficient building materials to a redeveloper, urban forest projects, and stream restoration projects.

Abex Corporation – Portsmouth, Virginia

The Abex Corp. Superfund site in Portsmouth, Virginia, has an industrial past, including 50 years of foundry operations paired with improper disposal techniques. In 1996, the EPA, Abex Corporation, the City of Portsmouth and the Portsmouth Redevelopment and Housing Authority reached an agreement to design and conduct cleanup and reuse activities at the Site. In 1999, a civil rights lawsuit alleged that the Washington Park Public Housing (WPH) Complex was knowingly built on contaminated property. A settlement in 2000 determined that the U.S. Department of Housing and Urban Development and the Portsmouth Redevelopment and Housing Authority would permanently relocate all WPH residents. After relocation, cleanup efforts that had stalled during resolution of this legal issue resumed. The community now benefits from a community health center, dental center, commercial facilities, a fire station and the Charles A. Fisher Memorial Academy, part of the Portsmouth Sheriff's Office, located on the cleaned up site.

2. Environmental Justice

The EPA recognizes that minority and/or low-income communities may be disproportionately exposed to environmental harms and risks. As a result, the EPA works to protect these and other communities burdened by adverse human health and environmental effects and has incorporated environmental justice as a priority throughout the EPA. Accordingly, the EPA maintains its ongoing commitment to the fair treatment and meaningful involvement of all people regardless of race, color, national origin, or income with respect to the development, implementation, and enforcement of environmental laws, regulations, and policies. More information is available on the EPA's Environmental Justice in Waste Programs website.

ENVIRONMENTAL JUSTICE

The EPA's 2010 *Interim Guidance on Considering Environmental Justice During the Development of an Action* discusses what constitutes "fair treatment" and "meaningful involvement."

"Fair treatment" means that no group of people should bear a disproportionate share of the negative environmental consequences resulting from industrial, governmental, and commercial operations or policies.

"Meaningful involvement" means that:
- People have an opportunity to participate in decisions about activities that may affect their environment and/or health;
- The public's contribution can influence the regulatory agency's decision;
- Their concerns will be considered in the decision-making process; and
- Decision makers seek out and facilitate the involvement of those potentially affected.

The EPA is committed to improving environmental performance through compliance with environmental requirements, preventing pollution, promoting environmental stewardship, and incorporating environmental justice across the spectrum of our programs, policies, and activities. When working with local environmental justice communities, the EPA encourages parties to:

- Meaningfully involve the community in the planning, cleanup, and revitalization process;

- Review the cumulative effects of multiple sources of contamination in close proximity to one another;

- Ensure an equitable distribution of brownfields assistance to potential environmental justice communities;

- Adhere to community commitments made in brownfields grant proposals;

- Assist potential environmental justice communities in obtaining independent technical advisors to help communities navigate the brownfields cleanup and redevelopment process;

- Provide equal opportunity for local minority-owned businesses specializing in environmental assessment and cleanup work to compete for contracts needed to plan, clean up, and revitalize brownfields; and

- Take steps to limit the displacement, equity loss, and cultural loss of the local community.

3.   **Public Participation**

Citizens are an essential component of the Superfund cleanup and RCRA permitting processes and the revitalization of these sites and brownfields sites. Formal public participation activities, required by law or regulation, are designed to provide citizens with both access to information and opportunities to participate in the cleanup process. The EPA uses the term "public participation" to denote activities that:

- Encourage public input and feedback;

- Encourage a dialogue with the public;

- Provide access to decision makers;

COMMUNITY ENGAGEMENT INITIATIVE: PUBLIC PARTICIPATION IN THE CLEANUP PROCESS

The EPA benefits from active participation of the public in the cleanup of contaminated sites. Effectively engaging communities means the EPA will need to make information easy to understand; find effective ways to reach the diverse public using a variety of communication tools and outreach efforts; find creative ways to respond to their needs and suggestions; and work with partners, stakeholders, and other federal agencies to make informed decisions to find the best solutions. Against this broad spectrum of activities, certain guiding principles provide consistency in developing a more robust community engagement process.

The EPA's guiding principles are to:

- Proactively include community stakeholders in the decision-making process;
- Make decision-making processes transparent, accessible, and understandable;
- Include input from a diversity of stakeholders throughout the cleanup process;
- Explain government roles and responsibilities; and
- Ensure consistent participation by responsible parties.

- Incorporate public viewpoints and preferences; and

- Demonstrate that those viewpoints and preferences have been considered by the decision makers.

In the revitalization context, working with a variety of community members, local planners, elected officials, and other stakeholders is an effective way to identify and integrate long-term community needs into reuse plans for the site. Redevelopment planning enables affected stakeholders to realize their vision for the future reuse of the site. This process should encourage participation of all community members in goal development, action planning, and implementation. By considering a community's vision of future land uses for contaminated sites, the EPA work with PRPs to accommodate community goals.

While successful redevelopment planning may occur at any stage of a cleanup, the planning process and community involvement should begin as early as possible. The planning process can last several days or months depending on the issues facing the community. It is vital to help communities think of, and participate in, long-term strategies for sustainable future land use.

4. Financial Assurance

Financial assurance requirements are implemented under CERCLA and RCRA to ensure that adequate funds are available to address closure and cleanup of facilities or sites that handle hazardous materials. Financial assurance requirements play an important role in promoting the revitalization of contaminated

South Point Plant – South Point, Ohio

From 1943 until the late 1990s, manufacturing facilities at the South Point site produced ammonium nitrate explosives, fertilizers, industrial chemicals, coal pitch pellets, ethanol, and liquid carbon dioxide. After cleanup, EPA Region 5 issued the first RfR Determination for industrial uses in the Midwest for the site in October 2004. Superfund cleanup and subsequent redevelopment of the site have transformed the area into a premier industrial park. In 2011, businesses at The Point employed approximately 320 employees and provided over $12.2 million in annual income to employees. Businesses cite the RfR Determination as one of the key factors in locating to the Site.

sites. Where financial resources are available for cleanup or closure activities, entities interested in reusing or redeveloping the property are not confronted with the question of where to obtain the resources for cleaning up the property. When there are inadequate financial assurance funds, the EPA or the states may have to spend taxpayer money to fund cleanups. This not only shifts the responsibility away from the liable party, it may also result in a significant delay in closure or cleanup activities. While the property awaits the performance of closure or cleanup activities, it is often difficult to attract outside parties to the property for further reuse and redevelopment.

C.   EPA Initiatives and Programs

1.   Brownfields Grants and State/Tribal Funding

The EPA implements a competitive grant program for the assessment and cleanup of brownfield sites, along with environmental job training under CERCLA § 104(k). The brownfields grant program provides direct funding for brownfields assessment, cleanup, and revolving loans (establishment of a revolving loan fund for eligible entities to make loans to be used for cleanup), which helps communities revitalize blighted sites by allowing them to take what is often the first step in the process -- addressing potential contamination.

To be eligible for a brownfields grant, the applicant must meet the statutory definition of an "eligible entity" and must plan to use the grant funding at a property that meets the definition of a "brownfield site." CERCLA §§ 104(k)(1), 104(k)(3), and 101(39). CERCLA defines a brownfield site broadly, but excludes certain sites from funding eligibility, e.g., based on their regulatory or ownership status. CERCLA § 104(k)(4)(B) imposes certain other restrictions on the use of brownfield grant funding, such as the prohibition on the use of funds to pay response costs at a site at which a recipient of the federal grant funds would be considered liable as a PRP. Because state and tribal response programs play a significant role in cleaning up brownfields, CERCLA also authorizes the EPA to provide assistance to states and tribes to establish or enhance their response programs. CERCLA § 128(a).

More information is available on the Brownfields and Land Revitalization program website.

2.   Superfund Redevelopment Initiative

The EPA's Superfund Redevelopment Initiative (SRI) helps communities return some of the nation's worst hazardous waste sites to safe and productive use. While cleaning up these Superfund sites and making them protective of human health and the environment, the EPA is working with communities and other partners in considering future use opportunities and integrating appropriate reuse options into the cleanup process.

At every cleanup site, the EPA's goal to make sure that the EPA and its partners have an effective process and the necessary tools and information to fully explore future uses before the cleanup remedy is implemented. This gives the EPA the best chance of making its remedies consistent with the likely future use of a site. In turn, the EPA gives communities the best opportunity to

Norwood PCBs – Norwood, Massachusetts

For almost 40 years, a succession of electrical equipment manufacturing businesses operated on and ultimately contaminated the Norwood PCBs Superfund site in Norwood, Massachusetts. Cleanup began in 1983. A local business owner entered into a PPA with the EPA in 1997 as part of his purchase of a 10-acre portion of the site. Now the site is home to two large buildings, totaling 56,000 square feet of commercial/retail space.

reuse sites in a protective and productive manner following cleanup.

More information is available on the Superfund Redevelopment Initiative program website.

3.   Sustainability and Green Remediation

Sustainability is commonly defined as the ability to maintain or improve standards of living without damaging or depleting natural resources for present and future generations and offers a framework to address such challenges. It takes into account the inherent linkages between environmental, economic and social conditions. Sustainable reuse of formerly contaminated sites is a multi-faceted, long-term approach that enhances environmental cleanup and protection with economically sound development practices and the promotion of social equity. Each regional office has its own "green" or "sustainable policy." Greener remediation is the practice of considering all environmental effects of remedy implementation and incorporating options to minimize the environmental footprint of cleanup actions.

Since 2004, OSRE has integrated sustainable and greener remediation principles into its core enforcement work such as the consideration of the five elements of a green cleanup assessment:

- Total Energy Use and Renewable Energy Use
- Air Pollutants and Greenhouse Gas Emissions
- Water Use and Impacts to Water Resources
- Materials Management and Waste Reduction
- Land Management and Ecosystems Protection

OSRE supports the inclusion of greener remediation and other sustainable provisions in its orders, agreements, and statements of work (SOWs), assists in renewable energy development on current and formerly contaminated land and mine sites when opportunities arise, and helps facilitate the appropriate reuse of contaminated property. More information may be found on the Green Remediation Focus website.

White Farm Equipment Co. Dump – Charles City, Iowa

On July 15, 2011, EPA Region 7 issued its first Ready for Reuse (RfR) Determination for the White Farm Equipment Co. Dump site in Charles City, Iowa. The RfR Determination states that the site is ready for a wide range of EPA-approved uses and was co-signed by the Iowa Department of Natural Resources. The site is now being leased for agricultural grazing. Wildlife resides in the adjacent wetlands.

4.   RCRA Brownfields Prevention Initiative

A potential RCRA brownfield is a RCRA facility that is not in full use, where there is redevelopment potential, and where reuse or redevelopment of that site is slowed due to real or perceived concerns about actual or potential contamination, liability, and RCRA requirements.

The RCRA Brownfields Prevention Initiative was established by the EPA to encourage the reuse of potential RCRA brownfields so that the land better serves the needs of the community, either through more productive commercial or residential development or as greenspace.

The initiative links the EPA's brownfields program with the EPA's RCRA corrective action program, other EPA cleanup programs, and state cleanup programs to help communities address contaminated and often blighted properties that may stand in the way of economic vitality.

The initiative includes:

- Showcasing cleanup and revitalization approaches through RCRA brownfields prevention pilot projects;

- Addressing barriers to cleanup and revitalization with targeted site efforts (TSEs);

- Supporting outreach efforts of the EPA's regional offices, states, and the RCRA community through conferences, training, Internet seminars, and the RCRA brownfields webpage; and

- Identifying policies that inadvertently may be hindering cleanup and addressing them with guidance, technical assistance, or other means.

5.   RE-Powering America's Land Initiative (Renewable Energy)

The EPA's RE-Powering America's Land Initiative encourages renewable energy development on current and formerly contaminated land and mine sites. This initiative identifies the renewable energy potential of these sites and provides a variety of resources for communities, developers, industry, state and local governments, or any other party interested in reusing contaminated or formerly contaminated land for renewable energy development.

More information is available on the RE-Powering America's Land website.

6.   Next Generation Compliance Initiative

As technology advances, the EPA is exploring new ways to exchange information, monitor sites, and further environmental protection. The EPA, states, citizens, and industry are moving towards real-time electronic information regarding environmental conditions and compliance. To maximize the uses of these technologies, the EPA is working on "Next Generation Compliance," which uses advances in information technology, increased transparency, and better-designed rules to improve environmental protection.

Next Generation Compliance has five components:

- Rulemaking – Designing and structuring rules and regulations to ensure greater compliance, such as including requirements for regulated entities to regularly assess their compliance;

- Technology – Using advanced emissions and pollutants monitoring technology, such as infrared cameras, for compliance monitoring so that regulated entities and the public are better informed about entities' pollution;

- Electronic reporting – Using modern information technology to transition from paper to electronic reporting of items such as permit data, compliance information, and enforcement actions;

- Transparency – Making both current and new entities' enforcement and compliance information, such as information obtained from advanced emissions and pollutants monitoring and electronic reporting, more publicly available; and

- Innovative enforcement approaches – Employing new or innovative enforcement approaches, such as including tools like advanced emissions and pollutants monitoring or electronic reporting requirements in the EPA's enforcement settlement agreements with entities.